I Love You Because I Love You

The Story of Love and Creative Perspective on Parenting a Child with Autism

Sharon Joyce S. Valdez
Hector Martin I. Valdez

Ukiyoto Publishing

All global publishing rights are held by

Ukiyoto Publishing

Published in 2021

Content Copyright © **Sharon Joyce S. Valdez & Hector Martin I. Valdez**

Cover by Martin Cross S. Valdez

ISBN 9789814989237

All rights reserved.
No part of this publication may be reproduced, transmitted, or stored in a retrieval system, in any form by any means, electronic, mechanical, photocopying, recording or otherwise, without the prior permission of the publisher.

The moral rights of the author have been asserted.

Names, characters, businesses, places, events, locales, and incidents are either the products of the author's imagination or experienced in person.

This book is sold subject to the condition that it shall not by way of trade or otherwise, be lent, resold, hired out or otherwise circulated, without the publisher's prior consent, in any form of binding or cover other than that in which it is published.

www.ukiyoto.com

Dedication

To Kuya Martin and Bunso Nicholas, you are our "Yin and Yang" and our home.

To our parents, you provide us with love and essential stimuli that make us strong and mindful.

To our siblings, you give us the reason to cherish our lives and live purposefully.

To our friends, your generous words of encouragement and true friendship keep us going.

To all who are helping us along the way, your gift of presence paves the way for more enlightenment and blessings for our family.

To all who seek answers to their autism journey and have the eagerness to see a different perspective, we share our stories and realizations with you.

To our God Almighty, You make all things possible. You lead and we follow.

FOREWORD

"I am different, not less."
- Mary Temple Grandin

Proponent of autism rights and neurodiversity
Inventor of the "hug machine"
Diagnosed with Autism Spectrum Disorder (ASD)

As one of the many individuals in the academic community, I have been oriented to the diversity of all learners. I have taught myself and formed the perspective of not looking at my learners based on what they can do and not what they cannot. However, I am just an outsider compared with the authors of this book. Their life journey with a child with ASD is far more different than my very limited education and exposure to the spectrum.

How do we face an unseen adversary?
What will we do to an incurable condition?
Who should we blame?
Where can we seek help?
When do we stop fighting?
Why does it have to be us?

This book is about the authors' challenging trek with their child with autism -- their pains, fears, frustrations, struggles, thoughts, aspirations, and experiments -- in their quest to seek answers to many of their questions. Furthermore, this book offers practical solutions to predicaments/dilemmas other parents face while taking care of their children with autism. All of these are based on the authors' observations, discoveries and experimentations that were anchored on existing literature and educational philosophies.

I may not know much about the spectrum but I have always been firm in my belief that all individuals are intelligent and capable in various ways. Hence, not less.

Maria Diwata V. Cadiente, LPT, MAEd
Professor, College of Teacher Education, Arts, and Sciences
University of La Salette, Inc.
Santiago City, Philippines

CONTENTS

Introduction	1
Chapter 1: Acceptance	9
Chapter 2: Love	16
Chapter 3: Patience & Grit	24
Chapter 4: Creativity & Resourcefulness	46
Chapter 5: Vigilance	59
Chapter 6: Resilience	67
Chapter 7: Gratitude	72
Chapter 8: Where Are We Now?	79
Appendix	*92*
About the Authors	*93*

Introduction

Bunso has Autism and It's Okay
by Mama SJ

I was about to take the Nursing Licensure Examination when I learned that I was pregnant with my second and youngest child. Honestly, it took me almost a month before I embraced the fact that I was again blessed with a precious gift and my dream of becoming a registered nurse and a psychiatric nurse would be postponed. I had a very sensitive first pregnancy and I was afraid to experience it again too soon. "Everything happens for a reason" as they say. I realized that God sent him to me because he would make my family more happy and complete. Kuya (our eldest son) was our only child for five years and his desire of having a baby sibling would make him the happiest boy in the world.

Like every parent's dream, I wished that Bunso (our youngest son) would be the best person that he ought to be. We claimed that he would be a beautiful person inside and out, perfect in the eyes of man as he or she would be perfect in the eyes of God.

Papa, Kuya, and I would always talk to my womb, saying all our wishes for Bunso like Papa and I did while I was conceiving Kuya. Every day was such a happy day for everyone despite being very challenging for me. I had to be a mom to Kuya and wife to Papa while experiencing another difficult pregnancy. My body was frail but I was surrounded with a dependable family, to whom I was getting my strength. Mom was with us and she was my companion while Papa was working.

During the second trimester, I noticed that Bunso seldom moved. I told myself, I hope he would be more subdued than Kuya, a quiet and peaceful boy as he grows. I experienced labor pains that were more painful and had a quick and easy delivery compared to my first but Bunso was diagnosed with poor hearing in his left ear. His pediatrician told us to have him checked again after six months. After six months, his hearing was fine.

While he was growing up, Bunso was jolly, active, receptive, and have all the characteristics of a normal growing kid that were age appropriate. He seldom got sick. We were glad to see that he was growing up having most of Kuya's traits.

But when he reached 24 months, we noticed that his development somewhat became slower than the usual. He started not to respond when being called, didn't have an eye contact during conversations, refused to be read with stories, refrained from playing educational toys, didn't learn words the way other kids learn like his age, tore books, threw toys frequently, didn't want to wear clothes at home, only wanted to eat certain foods repeatedly, fixated with turning the lights on and off, would open and shut doors frequently, fascinated with flowing water and fireworks, only wanted to watch a particular movie for days, and had excessive energy. Papa and I were teachers. We knew for a fact that something was wrong with him. Based on our own observation and assessment, we already had a hint that he might be having a Global Development Delay (GDD) but most probably, Autism.

We chose not to seek the help of a developmental pediatrician right away. We were hoping that as months would pass, Bunso's behavior and speech would improve. Then in June 2014, when Bunso was only three years old, we decided to set an appointment with the doctor who was referred by a friend. After six months of waiting and days before his fourth birthday, he finally had his initial assessment.

When the pediatrician informed us that Bunso was having the condition *Autism Spectrum Disorder (ASD), Mild*, we were not surprised. We were smiling while the doctor was saying her verdict and by the look on her eyes, she was surprised with our reaction. Maybe she was expecting us to get devastated and angry but we were not. We did not feel any sadness or frustration at all because ***"We love our son unconditionally and accept him for who he is despite his imperfections."***

"*May itatanong po ba kayo? (Do you have questions?),*" the doctor asked as if she was surprised with our positive reaction. Then Papa said, "*May mga hindi pa po ba kami naitanong, Doktora? (Are there questions that we aren't able to ask, Doctor?)*" Then the three of us laughed. We ended the conversation on a positive note.

We were thankful that our son would not take any medication. We were so glad that his locomotion was at par with his age and his cognitive skills was two years advanced his age. The doctor prescribed occupational therapy three times a week and speech therapy once a week to improve his behavior and language because both were a year and a half delayed. We were blessed that Bunso was considered highly functional.

On the day of Bunso's initial check-up we were able to meet someone from the occupational therapy center that was recommended by the doctor. We immediately visited the place. The interior, facilities, and environment were nice, warm, and conducive for learning. The staff was also very accommodating. The vibes were good. Bunso became at home immediately and we had an impression that he would surely love it there!

We saw big improvements on his behavior and speech (Take note, he did not start his speech therapy yet.) after five months of his regular OT sessions.

Now, he is able of respond when being called, engages in conversations with eye contact, follows simple commands, does simple tasks, becomes more affectionate, learns more words, likes storytelling and group playing, becomes more interested in books, tries to read on his own, is eager to show independence by preparing his own food, washing his own hands, keeping his own toys and clothes, and has wide food preferences. He loves being caressed with water that is why we let him enjoy the pool and he is not afraid of it. He is trying his best to swim and float on water. Eventually, when he is capable in understanding complex instructions, we will enroll him to formal swimming lessons.

Having an autistic child in the family is more challenging. He throws tantrums in public which makes us receive disgusted stares from people who do not understand and feel that we are bad parents. We cannot try different restaurants whenever we go to the mall because he only wants to eat ice cream and Jollibee Spaghetti. Everywhere we go, we are supposed to drop by the nearest SM Supermarket in our place because it is part of his fixations and routines. Bunso is very strict when it comes to his routines and gets frustrated easily when he is not able to do things as he wants it to be. As mentioned by the doctor, we should be watchful about these aspects, because our son is highly functional, can live on his own in the future and is capable of entering in a relationship. We have to teach him on how to deal with frustrations properly because a routinary person and a perfectionist like him may not be able to cope up when not guided accordingly.

All of us in the house, even Kuya, has to make sacrifices to make everything go smoothly because everything is unpredictable with Bunso. Just recently he does not want to watch movies anymore. He only wants to listen to music. Sitti Navarro and One Direction are the only artists that we hear for months and both calm him down. It is okay and advantageous to all of us because Papa and I want to limit him and Kuya's exposure to television and gadgets. He is very active and does not sit still for longer periods. We always chase him around the house and gets him down when he is climbing windows and cabinets. As a middle-class family, all of us should be conscious on how to use our financial resources. Bunso's therapy and needs are very, very expensive so we have to give up our personal wants just to make both ends meet. Through all these, ***we become extremely patient and giving.***

There are times when Kuya's asking, "Mama why is Bunso like that?" Then we explain to him again and again what condition his brother has and that we have to understand him more but not to the extent of spoiling him. Firmness should be exercised with gentleness. Bunso is intelligent. He knows how to get our attention and little by little he knows his limitations and understands whether he is doing something good or bad. To make Kuya understand his brother's condition, I always encourage him to read the story, "There's a Duwende in My Brother's Soup" by Lara Saguisag, whenever he is coming to the point that he is losing patience with him and it helps all the time.

Papa and I are afraid of the future despite the doctor's assurance and the experts say that Bunso is capable of living a normal life. All we have to do is believe that he can and guide him so that eventually he can go on with his life.

On the 6th of May 2015, Bunso had his follow-up check-up. The doctor told us that he was ready to attend SPED. She stressed out that it should be a special school and not a regular school. We told her that we had no intentions of forcing him to attend a regular school because it would hinder his growth and his classmates and teachers would suffer too.

We want him to study in a place where he deserves to be. We want him to soar high and reach his full potential in a school that fits him. We want him to be treated in a way that he is being understood. When he is already equipped with the necessary skills and behavior to fit in a regular school, then we will allow him to study there.

I believe that our acceptance and love for him make him improve in all aspects. At first, we were afraid that he would be treated indifferently by others due to the "stigma" of having Autism. But we asked ourselves, "Why should we listen to what other people would say?" We treat him and Kuya fairly. We treat Bunso like he has no special condition. ***He is okay. We are okay. He may be different from others, but for us he is a true blessing from the Lord.***

God gave us Bunso because right from the start He knew that we could take care of him and love him more than anyone else in this world.

Published in www.allaroundpinaymama.com on May 29, 2015

Chapter 1: Acceptance
by Mama SJ

"Love is the absence of judgment."
- Dalai Lama

Our family belongs to a line of academicians. You might be wondering how we communicate at home. The usual atmosphere during our family conversations is always anchored on sincerity, honesty, and objectivity. This line of thought is also applied to how we see and teach our kids. When Bunso was born, we immediately oriented ourselves in such a way that we would not repeat the same mistakes when we were raising Kuya. For example, we took note of what accessories were necessary, which brand of diaper, milk, food, and many others to consider. And since we are now aware of the probable milestones and achievements that might be exhibited by Bunso as he was growing up, we were very much observant to the habits that Bunso has exhibited as he was developing.

Early on, as we took note of the probable and expected milestones as Bunso was developing every month, we noticed many peculiar and "funny" antics that he was manifesting. For starters, we noticed that he literally "squirmed" like a worm before and during sleeping. We even called it "Uod (Caterpillar) Mode". We were happy and delighted by this antic of his. Added to this, we also observed that whenever we asked him to follow a "finger" or any moving object with his gaze, instead of following, he would usually smile and look at us. Of course, when he would smile at us, we would take it as a positive thing. As a toddler, he was fond of cars. Kuya gave Bunso his car collection when he was a boy. We would usually engage in a racing game wherein he would line up his cars on a racing track and we would spend time running after the cars that for some reason found their way to the most unholy places in the house. It was fun. On one occasion when all of us were resting together in the living room, we noticed that Bunso was lining up all the toy cars. When we tried to engage with him, he became hostile to the point that he would suddenly start hitting us while crying. Afterwards, there were many more instances when this behavior was observed. At that time, during one of our conversations when Bunso was around two years old, we shared together our observations. Other than the "lining-up" of cars and other objects and sudden tantrums, we also observed that Bunso would not say anything. He interacted with us by leading our hand or touching our face to direct us to what he wanted. We realized at that time that he was indeed not uttering any word. Furthermore, we also noticed that he kept on turning on and off all our light switches. He also had this habit of opening and closing the refrigerator door every time he would pass by the appliance. He also liked to take a bath every time he would go inside the bathroom to pee. We also noticed that he exuded extreme happiness whenever he would play with water and when it was raining. Other things such as repetitive acts like climbing on the window, running back and forth, closing and opening of drawers (that was why we removed all the doors of our cabinets), ripping off the pages of books and all labels of crayons, canned goods, and others. During that time, we also observed that he developed an erratic sleeping pattern. He also exhibited aversion to water consumption. This led him to drink only a specific brand of "orange juice". Another thing that occurred during that time was his fixation on watching "only" Japanese fireworks display videos on YouTube. There was also the habit of "excessive" nail biting and to top it all off, he started rejecting the idea of wearing clothes at home. Despite all our observations, we thought of observing more and reconfirmed if our observations were accurate. As parents and teachers, we believed that "the development of every individual is unique" and we have seen it with our students. A few days before his fourth birthday, we decided to bring our observations to a specialist.

Objectively speaking, we have seen similar cases of Bunso's habits. Before we even went to the specialist, we had our own conclusion of what might be his condition. With our observations, we made comparisons by reading literature and research on the habits exhibited by our son. We would usually exchange notes whenever we would encounter information on our observations. We even tried to look into our family background and traced similarities within our family lineage. During that time, our discoveries through our readings made us see our son's condition objectively.

When the developmental pediatrician informed us that Bunso was diagnosed with Autism Spectrum Disorder (ASD), we were not surprised at all. We were smiling while she was telling us her verdict. By the look in her eyes, she was surprised by our reaction. Maybe she was expecting us to get devastated and angry but we were not. We did not feel any sadness or frustration because we accept our son for who he is despite his imperfections. Our family treats him like we treat his Kuya. We deal with him as if he has no ASD so he lives his life confidently. He is who he is without any pretensions. We do not force him to do things that he is not ready doing. We are just there to guide him. Day by day, he surprises us as he improves and blooms. He does things confidently because we do not compare him with other kids. Like any other kid, he is unique. We encourage him to learn and not to compete with other kids. We teach him through words and actions that his greatest competitor is only himself and no one else. He has to conquer his fears, face his frustrations, celebrate his victories and we, his parents, are just there to guide, support, and cheer for him.

We remember what Bunso's occupational therapist said when we expressed our gratitude for making Bunso talk after three months of therapy, three times a week. He said that no matter how many times we would bring Bunso to therapy or how many interventions that he would take, Bunso's improvement would lie on the kind of mindset that we would exhibit. Being honest, open, rational, logical, and critical to our observations on how Bunso would develop as we worked with the therapists was according to him very crucial in coming up with the proper and essential intervention. He also emphasized that the presence and acceptance of the immediate family members, especially the parents were the crucial factors in the development of his condition. Looking back, we realized that by treating Bunso as we treated Kuya unbound by any biases and just plainly accepting him, enabled Bunso to open up to us and embraced us as part of his world while being confident for who he was.

Consequently, we have observed that even if people would sometimes ridicule him, he would just ignore them and still feel happy about the situation simply because we are there for him. There are no "ifs" or "whys" when we deal with Bunso. There is only the idea of looking forward to another adventure, another milestone, and a chance to be a better person. It is simply embracing the inevitable and look forward to the gift of togetherness that matter.

Accepting Bunso has paved the way for our family to find solutions to his concerns. Despite meeting some parents who tend to compare their children with Bunso, we are not affected at all. We believe that each person is unique and has his own pace of learning and readiness to explore new things. What applies to one may not apply to all. This notion makes me go back to the day when Bunso first experienced seeing a mascot and from then on has become traumatized in celebrating birthdays. Even just hearing the words "Happy Birthday" makes him anxious. One day, his schoolmate celebrated his birthday party in school and mascots were part of the celebration. Bunso was already experiencing sensory issues back then and the mere sight of too colorful huge mascots and loud sounds would create fear because they were too overwhelming for him. Every year, that kid would send invites a week before his birthday celebration and Bunso would remember his past experience. Bunso would ask us not to send him to school on that day and of course, we would not. Abrupt desensitization would not work for him and would just cause more trauma and anxiety on him. We know our child more than anyone else and we have already accepted it that one day, he would have his own time embracing the things that normal people do. It's plain and simple. Bunso is afraid of mascots at that point and we would never force him to love them immediately. We knew that he could overcome that fear according to his own pace and time.

For the last 10 years, Bunso is exhibiting a lot of peculiarities, likes, and dislikes. By accepting his uniqueness, he becomes more open and true to himself because he knows that he is being accepted by people who love him and they are always there to guide and support him as he grows. Like Bunso, we, who are considered by society as "normal" people, have also our own preferences that's why he is not different from us in this aspect. We also have our own readiness in certain aspects of our lives. Accepting Bunso is making him feel that he is not different from us and it is teaching him self-love and self-respect.

"Accept one another then, just as Christ accepted you."
Romans 15:7 NIV

Chapter 2: Love
by Mama SJ

"To a child, LOVE is spelled T-I-M-E."

- Zig Ziglar

In 2006, Papa and I decided that I should resign from work to take care of Kuya because it was the set-up that we realized that would work for our family. I gave up my teaching career to take care of him and when he was already a toddler, I went back to school, attending night classes and doing hospital duty during weekends hoping that when the time would come that he was already school-aged, I would pursue a Psychiatric Nursing career and return to the academe. But when I was about to take a review for the Nursing Licensure Examination, I got pregnant with Bunso. Setting aside my professional growth for the second time was inevitable but I finally accepted that being a full-time mom was indeed my mission and I should make the best out of it.

Being a stay-at-home mom is still the set-up that works for us that is forged on marriage as a partnership. Papa and I help each other in taking care of our family. As we nourish our relationship, we see to it that we should always consider our children as our top priority. Whenever they need us, we are always there for them because as Zig Ziglar believes, to a child love is spelled T-I-M-E.

If you are a working parent and you have a trustworthy and caring nanny to take care of your children, you are indeed very blessed. Even if you spend more time daily working for your family, please do not feel guilty but always be mindful that being a parent is more than just providing for your family. For us, we believe that it is the quality of time that you spend with your children that matters the most.

Being present physically is different from being present mindfully. Staying at home with our children is worthless if we are just there to exist. As parents, we should learn how to drop everything and attend to our kids in times when they need our attention. In our case, it is given literally that we should because Bunso has Autism Spectrum Disorder (ASD) and his Kuya needs us to better understand his little brother. Like for instance, our dear Bunso likes to do activities on his own and there are also activities that he likes to do with Papa, Kuya, and I separately. During weekends, his focus is solely on his Kuya and Papa because he knows that they have no school or work. These are the days when they play games and chat together. Bunso has the habit of feeling safe and secured by just staying beside them. When he feels that our time is not enough for him, he expresses this through "attention-seeking behavior" like having a tantrum or crying since he cannot express himself that well through words. Papa and I also see to it that we set a separate "dating day" with him and his Kuya. This is the time when we get to know our kids personally separately. In line with this, Papa has learned from a certain Bosconian priest during one of the retreats that he has attended that "parenting" is different from "herding" which has changed the way we communicate and spend time with our kids. Parenting is more personal while herding is leading the path to do things together as a family. To describe both in a simple way, having a meaningful conversation with each of our children is parenting while eating out together as a family is herding. Doing both creates happy memories that we want our children to keep and not scars that won't heal forever.

For two consecutive years, the years when Bunso was showing signs and symptoms of ASD which he was finally diagnosed of, Kuya would complain daily about his little brother's peculiar behaviors. He would ask us why Bunso would not like to play or converse with him, why he would not like to be hugged and kissed, why he would eat only "chicken barbecue" and drink "orange juice" every day, why he was lining up cars and would not like to wear clothes at home, etc.? Papa and I would patiently explain to him how he should approach his little brother because having six years of age gap was difficult for Kuya to adjust despite having him prepared for Bunso's coming. Maybe, his expectations were different from reality. Bunso exhibiting ASD was a different story. It would require Kuya to understand complicated concepts about his brother and how he would deal with those complexities at a very young age were indeed too heavy on his part. He was just a Kindergarten student when his little brother was born. We knew that it was hard for him and he felt that he was not a good Kuya when he could not even hug or kiss his little brother because Bunso found his touch too rough due to his sensory issues. With prayers and God's grace, I guess also due Kuya's love for his brother, he was eager to enter his world to understand him finally and Bunso reciprocated his gesture. Guess what Kuya has started doing recently to keep his constant communication with Bunso? They have "Roblox" time together daily as a form of their love language. By engaging with Bunso through Roblox, he is always able to communicate with him via his "virtual world" and the social and communication skills that he learns from that virtual world extend to Kuya's "real world". Through Roblox, Kuya has the capacity to go to his world, which according to Raun Kaufman, former CEO of Global Education for the Autism Treatment Center of America and author of Autism Breakthrough, is the first step in order to get the attention of a child with autism. Roblox, by the way, is a global gaming platform where millions of people from all ages and walks of life gather together every day to imagine, create, and share experiences with each other in immersive, user-generated 3D worlds.

In line with this, generally based on experience, a child with ASD may exhibit a "photographic memory" that is why we are always mindful with how we behave and speak at home. Like for instance, "mirroring" works for Bunso. He shows back what we show him so we always do our best to be loving and caring so that he will do the same to us. In short, when we deal with Bunso, we reap what we sow. He is like a sponge. What you teach him, he absorbs and he does. Literally, Bunso is a representation of all the people inside our home.

There was a time when Papa and Kuya went in our hometown to celebrate the holidays with my in-laws. Bunso knew that they would stay there for a couple of weeks and giving them the exact date when they would come back mattered to him. He was counting the days and got more and more excited as the date of their return went near. Unfortunately, Kuya and Papa were not able to return as promised. Since Bunso was exhibiting "rigidity", he could not easily accept the fact that he would not see the boys as promised. He was hurt deep inside but could not explain or express explicitly. I was able to process the matter with him but it left a mark on his memory. As the boys entered our home when they arrived, Bunso was crying profusely saying that he was sad and asking them why they did not come back home as promised. Therefore, more than the absence of the person that he holds dear greatly affects his behavior but breaking a promise affects him more. Fulfilling a promise is an act of love for him that is why after that incident, we religiously fulfill what we say. Bunso has taught us that promises should not be broken because it leaves a feeling of untrustworthiness and unimportance. Through that experience, we never give him "false hope". We choose what we say to him. We do not make promises as much as possible but when we do, we make ample time for our promises to be fulfilled. Giving him surprises instead of promises also works for him. It leaves a lasting happy memory and he feels important when we do.

Bunso was fidgety and his attention span was very short before. He would also manifest uncontrollable mood swings, tantrums, and more often, meltdowns. He would zone out, do repetitive movements, scream on top of his lungs, cry uncontrollably, stay still and stiff, hit us, or hurt himself. We found out that these behaviors all boiled down to one thing. He needed to fulfill his sensory issues. What we did when any of these behaviors would happen was to let him satisfy his urge to release his stress and anxiety, process the situation when he was calm already, and do touch therapy. Hard massages, hugs, and kisses would soothe him which made it a daily routine for us. Touch therapy became a huge factor in helping him alleviate his feelings that he could not express verbally.

I guess that he sees all that we do as acts of love. As years pass, he becomes more and more affectionate, sweet, and loving. His "attention-seeking behaviors" diminish little by little.

There was one time when Papa asked him, "Bunso, why do you love me?" We were surprised when he answered, "I love you because I love you." I guess it means that for Bunso, love needs no explanations, no buts, no ifs. For him, love is love, plain and simple. For him, both the quantity and quality of time that we give him are acts of love and he does his very best to reciprocate by being the most sweet and affectionate little boy that he is right now.

How will I forget the memory that happened on the 29th of September 2017? Bunso woke up early that day and asked me if we could paint. Of course, I said yes! I guided his hand in doing soft strokes in creating his requested "fireworks". Then I had to turn off the stove because I was cooking breakfast. When I came back, he was giggling and showed me what he did. He wrote the words "I LOVE YOU" all by himself and he told me that he wanted to decorate his masterpiece with hearts and stars. I could not control my tears. Tears of joy perhaps because for the very first time, he tried his best to show his love and affection for me through art which he could not express through words. A moment like that has shown me how much God loves me. I may be experiencing struggles, doing more sacrifice, and adjusting to the needs of Bunso like other moms who have kids with special needs. At the end of the day, I know that there is a reason why God has given me Bunso. Perhaps He knows that I can love him unconditionally. Yes, I can and I do truly. I am so glad that he loves me too beyond words can express.

To Bunso, I love you more and more each day, my son! Thank you for being my baby.

"Let love and faithfulness never leave you;
bind them around your neck, write them on the tablet of your heart."

Proverbs 3:3

Chapter 3: Patience & Grit
by Papa Hector

"Patience is not the ability to wait but the ability to keep a good attitude while waiting."

- Joyce Meyer

When Bunso was diagnosed with ASD, the realities of our situation did not immediately dawn on us. Yes, we accepted his "gift" with open arms. We embraced his intricacies and we all agreed in the household to forge ahead with our decision with a firm resolution. As days went by, our understanding of his condition was supplemented with our experiences as teachers and through the readings that we did. We used to compare notes, we even adopted methods and procedures that were "proven effective" in many of the research that we read. To be honest, Bunso's condition made us explore more and push ourselves to learn a whole new world of habits, jargons, theories, and practices. On paper, many strategies would seem to look fantastic and effective. But later, we realized that there was more to it than mere executions and strategies.

MISSION 1: First Words

Many of the literature that we learned of our son's condition stated various manifestations that might be observed. Since Bunso, was "non-verbal", a condition wherein a child is unable to express in words everything in his mind, his method of communication was very limited. On top of this, his fine-motor skills (grasping, writing, holding, and manipulating things by hand) was very delayed. His therapist always emphasized the importance of "home-school collaboration" (HSC), a method wherein the activities done in school "must" be continued at home by the primary caregiver of the child who has special needs. As teachers, we were aware of the objectives of HSC, which was to create "consistency" in the learned experiences of the child which might lead to the development of functional habits. In the early stages of Bunso's therapy after his diagnosis, the primary target of the therapy sessions was to enable or teach him a method of communication. The therapist emphasized that since Bunso was having delayed auditory development (he was actually deaf when he was born), he had problems recognizing "sounds" which was the foundation of speech. The delayed development of his auditory process apparently prevented him from easily recognizing and differentiating sound. Bunso's pediatrician told us before that the "sense of hearing" would be the first sense that would develop during the child's development inside the womb. In the case of Bunso, since he could not hear anything when he was inside, he did not develop his sense of hearing.

Looking back, we had no idea what the task that Bunso's therapist was asking us to do. The very first activity that the therapist told us to do was to familiarize him with the basic letters of the alphabet, numbers, shapes, and colors. So, what we did was to fill the house with letter charts, activity books, visuals, and even videos. Then we immersed ourselves with the task at hand. Doing it was easier said than done. Since he could not speak and had no idea what we were saying, the mere task of asking him to sit down and learn the alphabet was an ordeal in itself. His therapist had constantly emphasized to us that "teaching" him was not similar to teaching regular students since he was aware that we were teachers. "Different" was not enough to describe the process. His attention span was close to none. The only good thing that we observed was that for some reason, he would respond to his name. He would usually look at us whenever we would call his name. His Kuya gave him his nickname. Since he would not sit still and was always roaming around the house, we placed letter, number, and shape charts on his route around the house. Then all of us agreed that every time he would pass by a chart, whoever was near the chart must call his name, then after he would respond to his name we would point at a particular "letter or number" then followed by the name of the symbol. We practiced one letter, number, and shape per week. Other than this, one hour before bedtime, we would read him a story book and another one upon waking up. We did it every day. By the way, during the times that he was awake, all of us in the house agreed not to use any gadget. No phone, laptop, PC, and even television since he was easily distracted by sound. One more thing, when we read to him a story, we would always point at the words and pronounce them clearly. We would even hold his hand and guide his fingers as we read the story. At the same time while reading, we would read it aloud and with emotions while looking at him. We would even ask him questions regarding the story and of course we were also the ones who would answer our own questions. As time went on, the number of story books for kids that we read to him increased. Three months after his therapy he spoke. It happened on a weekend when we had a visitor in the house. Our guest brought with them their daughter who was a year older than Bunso. Her name was "Dumpling" (not her real name). At that time, there was a trending TV advertisement which had a tagline, "Sino ang best friend mo doon? (Who is your best friend?)" After the visit we asked him out of jest, "Eh sino ang best friend mo roon? (Well, who is your best friend?)" We were not expecting any answer to that question since Bunso never answered any of our questions. To our surprise, he answered,

"Eh 'di si Dumpling! (Well, it's Dumpling!)" It took us seven months to hear those words from him. By the time he spoke those first words, we have been reading 45 books, seven times a day, seven days a week.

MISSION 2: Becoming Flexible

On Winnie the Pooh cartoons, there was a character named "Rabbit". His main attribute was his "rigidity" in doing things. Two of the characteristics of Bunso being a child with ASD and Attention Deficit and Hyperactivity Disorder or ADHD (He was diagnosed with ADHD when we sought for second opinion.) were his rigidity and consistency in following procedures. This means that when doing things, we should follow the "EXACT" same procedure. These include the same route, color, food, time, and would you believe shape, size, and color.

We used to buy our grocery every day. By the way, we happen to live in a house wherein the supermarket is located on the ground floor. Around 300 meters from our house to the supermarket, there are three routes going to the area. One of the key tasks that we needed to fulfill for the HSC was to expose Bunso to people, crowded places, and different locations. So, every time we would go to the supermarket, we would always tag him along. During our first trip with him to the area, we followed the longest route. We took our time to roam around the area, looking at every lane and exposing him to the different objects in the supermarket. As we walked along, we named the objects especially the ones that he would always eat. Our first trip was a success. The following day at around the same time when we did the trip to the supermarket, he started pestering us to dress up saying repeatedly, "Bihis na, Papa." Finally, we did make the trip, but the problem was, he wanted to follow the same route and he even wanted us to walk on the same order while we went to the supermarket. We also repeated roaming around the place and he even asked us to identify the same objects. At first, we were so happy since he remembered the specific details of our previous trip. But then afterwards, he wanted to repeat the same routine every day. It even increased to two trips per day. We followed the same route, same sequence, bought the same food brand and flavor (ice cream, strawberry lollipop, chips), and would you believe, he had to wear the same shirt? That routine persisted for six years. Along the way, we developed a system that would enable us to cope with the demands of his routine.

Other than the supermarket, he also had a routine at home. He would follow a specific path when he roamed around the house. He would usually roam around, turning on and off all the light switches as well as opening and closing doors and drawers every 15 minutes. Another one was his eating routine. He would only eat the food if the number of food elements was three. Three pieces of chicken, three eggs, three servings of rice, three scoops of ice cream. He would feel hungry every two hours and for six years, his only viand was "chicken barbecue". Breakfast, lunch, dinner, and even snacks… chicken barbecue and orange juice. For entertainment, same Kdrama title and episode with a volume of 12. We developed a very keen sense of hearing and we were able to learn to do lip reading since we could not hear the sound of the TV program that we were watching (wink). Before bedtime, he would ask for a hard massage from head to toe for almost two hours every day.

Dealing with the rigidity of Bunso due to his uniqueness has really tested every aspect of our family. During those times, we just could not accept that just going along with the flow would solve the problem. So, we thought of ways on how we might be able to change or tone down his rigid behavior. We believed that habits might be developed through practice and repetition since human behavior might be developed based on patterns of activity and stimuli. We hypothesized that if we would introduce certain patterns of behavior and do it repetitively just like how we taught him to read, then we might be available to change Bunso's rigid behavior.

The first thing that we did was to identify the pattern of behavior or the triggering act that would make him do a particular action. For example, the rigid route going to the supermarket, we noticed that there were certain words that would trigger his impulse to make the trip. Words such as food, dinner, breakfast, *pasalubong* (souvenir), surprise, *libot* (to roam around) were banned during conversations. All of us in the household agreed to it. We noticed that his tendency to ask us to go to the supermarket was lessened to a certain degree.

Other than banning certain words, we also created guidelines on how to properly prepare him when we were about to go out of the house. These included refraining from informing Bunso about an activity. Everyone was strictly forbidden within the household to talk about any activity or future plan that would involve "going out". Furthermore, on the day of the actual "activity", all family members who would be going out were to prepare in advance before Bunso was informed of the nature of the activity. He was the last to get dressed. Why? Because if he was informed of the activity ahead of time, he would start asking everyone in the household "when are we gonna go?" The catch was that if we would not answer him then he would conclude "Let's go na Papa!" He would repeat the same question all day even to the extent of approaching us one by one to ask the same question while staring us directly in the face while holding our heads.

Another thing that we adhered to is the act of setting the itinerary, goals, objectives, and expectations for the trip and activity. We would usually begin by telling him the itinerary including the places that we would be visiting, the route (this is very important) that we would be taking, and the alternatives that we might include in our itinerary. Afterwards, we would review the itinerary and would emphasize what we should do and the reason why we should go to that place. Then, we would tell him what he needed to do. These included his expected behavior and why he would need to do it. After doing all these things then we would cap it by telling him the "rewards" that he would receive and what people would think of him. We emphasize on "positive reinforcement" by giving him a hug, kiss, and praises for doing the job well. We noticed that by providing positive reinforcement and subtle criticisms, Bunso was able to develop his own self-worth. We also observed that he became more receptive and proactive in doing things. He also started to take the initiative in doing things. One example was when he would include his own "grocery list" by doing it on his own. He would also help in doing the shopping and even pushing the cart. We also realized that he started interacting with the people in the supermarket by mimicking the way we would respond to the supermarket personnel. At first, he was only mirroring our behavior and even our words. What we would always do was whenever he would exhibit a polite expression, we would always explain to him in simple words why we needed to be polite, nice, and appreciative of other people. If you are wondering how he would react to our simple explanation, he would not exhibit any reaction. Kuya would usually ask us if his brother was able to understand us. In all those times that we explained things to Bunso and he would not respond, we would tell Kuya that even if he would not respond, the most important thing was that he would hear it coming from us and that when we would talk to Bunso normally as we would talk to a friend. The most important thing that we always emphasized was that we had to do it consistently and that we needed to first call Bunso's attention by calling his name then we would look at him at eye level then in a calm voice we should explain to him things that he needed to learn. It took us four years before he learned to look at us and listen to what we were saying.

Changing our itinerary or schedule was one of the most challenging things that we had to hurdle of Bunso's rigidity. We started with following the usual route and schedule. The thing was, after we fulfilled his routine then that would be the time when we would talk to him and "suggest" an activity that we needed to do before we went home. We started with one suggestion. Then as time went on, we added more. The "suggestions" developed a habit of anticipation wherein it came to a point where he would expect that there might be a probable change or addition in our itinerary. Afterwards, we tried changing the sequence of our itinerary. For example, if in the past we used to fulfill his routine then did something else later, we re-arranged it in such a way that we would do all the "other" things first like going to the bill payment section then to the bank, meet someone, and other things that were not part of his routine. Well of course it was not easy. There were times that he would throw a tantrum. At some point he had a grand meltdown in the middle of the supermarket. There was even a time when he was having a major meltdown. While we were waiting for him to calm down as he was rolling on the floor of the supermarket and shouting at the top of his voice, we were approached by the security personnel of the mall and we were asked what we were doing to Bunso. Public tantrums and meltdowns were his thing before. In all those times, we stood our ground and waited for him to calm down and then afterwards we explained to him slowly the things that he did. If you're wondering how we felt at that time, in the beginning, we felt bad, ashamed, embarrassed, humiliated, and many more adjectives synonymous to the words that I have mentioned. His therapist at that time had greatly stressed to us the importance of learning the correct approach and attitude in addressing such events. We learned that since Bunso had a problem in communicating his feelings to people, it was important for us as his companion to instill in him the value of "trust". Developing trust could not be explained through words alone. We learned that we had to show and explain it to him slowly and consistently. From the tone and volume of our voice, facial expressions, gestures, and body language, we should express to him that we were there to wait for him and that we would understand. During those times we stopped minding the people around us and instead only focused on him. Patience, love, and utmost focus on Bunso aided by our consistent processing of his behavior in public enabled him to realize that no matter what he would do, we would patiently wait for him to come around. Furthermore, he also realized that if he would exhibit unpleasant behavior in public, he would not be able to get what he wanted. One of the key points in Bunso's development was the consistent and repetitive reinforcement of his behavior. Since his condition would allow him to take everything at face value, we realized that it was essential to explain or teach him repetitively the "reason" why we do things like behaving properly and doing things the right way based on a set rule. One more thing, we realized that it was very important to teach him properly since he would not forget the things that we would teach him. Bunso "mirrors" not only our words but also our behavior and reasoning. Mirroring is one of the characteristics of children with Autism.

MISSION 3: Conquering "Echolalia"

One of the distinct characteristics of children with ASD is repetitive vocalization of words uttered by other people known as *"**echolalia**"*. In some cases, a child with ASD may repeat his own words. This is known as *"**palilalia**"*. Guess what, Bunso has exhibited severe cases of both conditions. Imagine talking to a live recorder who repeats everything that you say or repeats words, or phrases over and over again.

Three months after Bunso started having his Occupational Therapy (OT) sessions, he started talking. We were so happy when Bunso started mimicking our words. We thought it was funny and frustrating since Bunso just repeated everything. Logic and reasoning were irrelevant. We were at a loss on how to address it. We tried explaining to him that he must not repeat our words. Well, it didn't work. At that time, we decided to learn more about his condition. After consulting with his therapists and learning from books and present research on his condition, we learned that echolalia exhibited by children with ASD carry a wide range of meaning anchored to their needs. To address Bunso's condition, we observed that he exhibited echolalia and palilalia on certain occasions.

For ***echolalia***, we observed that he would repeat our words when he wanted to get or do something. Like that time when we were eating together, Kuya asked him "Bunso, what do you like?" Bunso replied "Bunso, what do you like?... What do you like?... What do you like?" Kuya then asked him,

"Do you like rice?" to this question. He did not reply. Then afterwards, Kuya asked "Do you like water?", to this he replied "Do you like water?... Do you like water?... Do you like water?" We offered him a glass with water which he took and drank. We saw the same behavior every time he wanted to request something and when he agreed to what we were saying. We also observed that it was his way of saying "yes". Other than echolalia, Bunso also had the habit of repeating his own words (***palilalia***). It would come in the form of a word, phrase, or sentence. Back then whenever we were preparing to go to his favorite place, the "supermarket", he would usually say "Let's go to the *Sukermarket*... market... market... market... market..." He would repeat it over and over again until we would say otherwise. By the way, the word "Sukermarket" was not a typo. That was Bunso's way of pronouncing supermarket when he was four years old. Sometimes he would repeat a phrase or a line from a movie clip that he watched on the internet for days.

There were many techniques and methods that we learned on how we would help Bunso overcome echolalia and palilalia. What we learned from our trials was that some methods might not necessarily work all the time. For Bunso's condition, what we found effective was to teach him the proper method of expression then afterwards provide him the reason and rationale of the action or expression. For example, back then whenever he wanted to drink water he would say "Bunso, would you like some water?" He would request for a cup of water by saying his name and asking a question. Every time he would say this, we would say "Bunso, (*eye level in a soft manner of speech*) you say, "Can I have some water?" We would allow him to repeat the question and we would guide him to direct the question from us. Then we would follow-up by asking him "Why do you like to drink water?" Then we would provide him with an answer. We would start by saying "I want to drink water because…" We would also provide the reason why. It was a slow and tedious process of habit formation. We realized that Bunso's reasoning skills improved through the years as he matured and as we exposed him to movies and stories about human interaction. Six years after he was diagnosed with his condition, the habit of echolalia and palilalia has greatly reduced. He can now provide reason for his actions, though at times we still correct him. Our small steps and consistent efforts in prodding him to think for himself and understand the reason for his actions and why he needs to do certain things has made a lot of difference. We technically have learned to "echo" the "correct or right" information to him and use the condition of "repetitive action" to inculcate the things that we want him to do and we think is necessary for him to learn. We've learned that since he repeats his words and actions, we have hypothesized that we can utilize it to instill in him the proper behavior, reasoning, and habits that may be of help to him to become self-reliant. Of course, we've realized too that we have to be very careful of the things that we teach and be very vigilant with the information that we provide and expose him to since he absorbs and remembers vivid sensory inputs.

MISSION 4: Expanding His Food Choices

The most challenging aspect of Bunso's development was his food preference. We grew up in a traditional household. One of our most cherished past time was to try new food dishes. When Bunso came to us, that changed completely. When he was four years old, we noticed that his sensory issues also included a particular preference to a certain type of food that had a particular taste, texture, and smell. There was a time when his preferred viand was "chicken barbecue". Imagine, he would eat his breakfast, lunch, and dinner, including after meal snacks with the same viand. During his fifth birthday, we prepared a simple celebration. Kuya back then requested for it and during our meal together his Kuya even helped in preparing his meal. Bunso back then was so happy because his Kuya prepared his meal. Afterwards, he started requesting for "chicken barbecue". The dish was a very simple mixture of chicken breast or thigh marinated in a locally made barbecue marinade. A dash of salt and pinch of ground pepper plus water was added. We would allow the mixture to boil until the water dries up. Then about a tablespoon of oil would be added. We would allow it to be slightly roasted until it caramelized to mimic the look of flame roasted chicken. Sometimes we would use the turbo broiler to roast it (if we had lots of time). At first it was okay but when it stretched for months and eventually turned into years, we were so worried. We tried introducing a variety of food to him but to our dismay he would always say "Papa/Mama, chicken barbecue lang". It was frustrating because we had to share and accompany him when he ate since we wanted him to learn proper manners. We hypothesized again that maybe when he would start to mature then we could gradually introduce other food items, then he would probably learn to like them. For our strategy, we became more consistent in accompanying him during his meals. Then we would always make it a point to let him see us eating a different type of food. We never invited him to taste what we were consuming but what we emphasized to him was the idea of how it tasted and we made him see that we enjoyed eating not only chicken barbecue. We also made additions to his chicken barbecue. We gradually intensified the spices used. We increased the amount of pepper and other herbs, we also used different preparations of barbecue sauces. Eventually he started to become curious and adventurous in his food preferences. It took us five years to expand our menu to what it is now and for Bunso to try other dishes. We realized that the key point in our success in making Bunso try other dishes other than chicken barbecue was "sensory integration". We observed that Bunso's change was due to two factors. One was his readiness and maturity and the other was the fulfilment of his sensory needs. By introducing him repetitively to the different taste stimuli, which would have various degrees of intensity, he became accustomed or familiar to the taste. We never forced him to do it. We just fulfilled his sensorial needs gradually which perhaps might have created the opportunity for him to see how our world looks like or rather tastes like.

MISSION 5: Making Eye Contact

One of the most pronounced characteristics of children with autism is their inability to make eye contact. Bunso never made eye contact with us when he was younger. No matter what we did, he never made eye contact. At first, we tried asking him "Bunso, look at Mama/Papa when you're talking to me/us." At times we would hold his chin and move it towards us to emphasize that he had to look at us when we were talking. During those times when we tried to ask or force him to make eye contact, we noticed that he became extremely agitated. One of his therapists emphasized that we had to remind him to look at us and at times hold his chin so that he would learn how to do it. But due to his agitation whenever we reminded him or forced him to look at us, we thought that probably it was not the proper method that would make Bunso learn to make eye contact. Back then we thought that it was hopeless until we came across a Facebook post which was posted by a high school student who was also with autism. She narrated her feelings whenever she was asked to make eye contact, sit-up straight, avoid fidgeting, or some other stuff that "normal kids" were supposed to do. She said that she felt so stressed whenever people asked her to do it. That popped up article made us think that Bunso might be the same that was why he would usually exhibit agitation or restlessness that usually led to tantrums and meltdowns. The answer to our problem came from Mr. Raun Kaufman. He was the former CEO of the Autism Treatment Center of America, an inspirational speaker and most importantly he was diagnosed with severe autism when he was young. According to him, the key to making kids with autism to learn things is for us "normal people" to enter in their world and be part of it. Once a child with autism has learned that we are a part of his world then that would be the time that they become receptive to the learning that we want them to have. In the case of eye contact, he said that to enable the child with autism to learn it we should make it a point to talk to him at eye level. Furthermore, the manner of speech should be calm and reassuring, not too loud, not too soft. We tried it with Bunso. Whenever we would talk to him, we have made it a point to speak with him at eye level. Then we have avoided forcing him to look at us. We also stopped asking him to "Look at me Bunso." We would just talk as if he was looking at us.

You might be wondering how it's like to talk with someone who may be perceived as "not paying attention"? Well, honestly it was annoying at first. But we just did it. We made it a point to emphasize and repeat the things that we would say to Bunso even if he was moving around as if we didn't exist. Two years after, we noticed that he would glance at us at times. Nine years after, Bunso now talks to us like a normal person. In fact, many people are usually surprised to learn that Bunso has autism whenever we tell them that he has a condition. This may be due to his friendly, affectionate, and sociable disposition. For nine years, we have learned to talk to ourselves, ask and answer our own questions while talking to him.

The Struggle

It may sound funny but it's not. We are not perfect. We also have days when we are so tired that we become very impatient. There were days in the past that we had to stay late to finish our deadlines or work on unfinished chores because that was the only time that Mama and I had for ourselves then Bunso would not cooperate or sleep early. We experienced this for months only to find out that it was related to sensory issues. As suggested by his developmental pediatrician, a full body massage might fix the problem. Then it worked! We remember the days when he could not go to school due to sleeping late and worse, he would become grumpy the whole day due to lack of sleep. Our family schedule and usual routines would be greatly affected negatively. Due to the body massage, he would seldom sleep late or wake up in the middle of the night and has already followed a regular sleeping pattern.

One of the characteristics of children with ASD is they are routinary and become agitated when their routines are not being followed rigidly. There were stages in Bunso's life when he would kiss each family member goodbye not just when we would go out of the house but also when we would go to the bathroom. Even if we sneaked out, he would know and he would knock at the door and he would not stop until he would be able to kiss us. He also had this fixations and routines on where to sit during meals or what utensils must be used on a particular dish. There was also his fixation of always checking on our "pantry" every time he would pass by the area. There was also the turning on and off of light switches. Each one was a challenge and an opportunity, or shall we say a "teachable moment" that lead us to guide him to becoming a better version of himself.

There are routines that we have removed and there are still a lot of them that we have not yet. Whenever we feel frustrated, we would always look at Bunso lovingly and say to ourselves, "He is our son. We love him. He is beyond all the challenges and trials that we experience. We will always look at him as he is. We will focus only to him and not on the things that he does that test our patience. We will do all these out of love." Indeed, patience made our marriage stronger, made us mature to be better parents, enabled us to always see beyond the problem and look for another perspective.

"But as for you, be strong and never give up, for your work will be rewarded."

2 Chronicles 15:7

Chapter 4: Creativity & Resourcefulness
by Us

"To live a creative life, we must lose our fear of being wrong."
- Joseph Chilton Pearce

Bunso is under the supervision of his therapists and special education teachers for five years before we decided to homeschool him under a provider and incorporate his occupational therapy activities on his subjects or *activities of daily living* (ADL) at home. We still remember the time when he was diagnosed with Autism Spectrum Disorder (ASD). He was non-responsive, speechless, rowdy, and impatient. He would usually throw tantrums, shout, or cry restlessly, or would not stay in one place for a long time both in private and public. Due to his routinary behavior and volatile temper, we would end up physically and emotionally exhausted at the end of each day.

The memory of him of being very excited to go to school to learn with his teachers and classmates is still vivid. It is a good memory. In his stay in

Cerecare Philippines Foundation, Bunso was well taken-cared of and being loved by his therapists and teachers. We could not ask for more. During those times, aside from dealing with Bunso's wholistic development, we encountered financial difficulties along the way but his teachers and therapists even the school administrations and owner were there to understand our pressing situation. Bunso's therapy sessions, education, and daily expenses were expensive. It was never easy and will never be easy to support a child with special needs. In short, our family knew that other families with members having special needs were also experiencing huge changes when talking about family mechanics and setting priorities.

We are so blessed that our dear Bunso belongs to the upper spectrum which means that he is highly functional. His hyperactivity is encompassing but he learns fast and adapts well to his environment. We are so glad that he can now express himself through words and actions, not that much developmentally appropriate yet but he is doing his best to communicate with us. He can follow instructions, has become more affectionate, has started engaging in interactive play, reads words, writes numbers and letters, draw simple objects, identify things, and helps at home.

We must say that the people we know who usually do not see him often observe positive changes in him or see him do antics that kids like his case do but it's okay. What we consider important is we keep on supporting him and guiding him to reach his full potential. As days come and go, each step with him becomes more challenging but it boils down to four things on how we manage the situation. First, *WE ACCEPT HIM FOR WHO HE IS*. We do not compare him with other kids. We know that he is unique like the rest of us. Our genuine acceptance and openness with his condition, we believe, makes him acceptable for most people. Second, *WE TREAT HIM NORMALLY*. We do not give him special treatment. We talk to him and deal with him like we do to the other members of our family. Third, *WE BELIEVE THAT HE CAN*. Like any person, may be normal in our societal standards or with special needs, we know that he can live a normal life independently and he can be successful in anything that he chooses to be in the future.

One of the things that we encourage him to do is to follow his passion according to his own pace. We do not pressure him. As suggested by a psychologist friend, we make sure that he is included in planning his own activities. By doing these, he feels that he is in control thus, he is more motivated in doing and finishing his tasks on time. He is now into playing educational games, solving easy and difficult puzzles (Yes, he can solve puzzles that adults here at home cannot.), painting, reading story books for children, and helping do the chores especially baking that he truly loves doing. Homeschooling works for him at this point and we are doing it for two consecutive school years already. It lets him see that studying is a way of life, not a separate endeavor from normal everyday living.

They say that homeschooling is more difficult and less expensive. In our case, yes, because we are doing it spontaneously by focusing on what truly matters and what Bunso really needs. We apply what former Xavier School San Juan Director, Father Johnny Go, has taught us, "Minimize activities, maximize impact" (MAMI). It does not only speak about our choices of activities for Bunso but also maximizing the materials that should be used. We are so blessed that nowadays there are many learning resources that we can find on the internet to support this. We can also maximize the use of our existing materials at home because we want Bunso to always incorporate his academics with real life situations. "Subject integration", a teaching strategy that focuses on one activity but taps more than one subject, is one of our favorite techniques. It saves time, effort, and resources but the impact is long-lasting.

Making Him Learn Baking

One of the things that we would like Bunso to learn is doing chores at home. The skills that he would learn could lead to his independence in the future. We are not going to live forever. As parents, we do not want his Kuya to be burdened when we are gone although we are so blessed to know that Kuya would not leave Bunso and would take care of him as he said. This is a relief, actually.

Bunso is always motivated to help at home especially in the kitchen. Then we discovered that he would enjoy baking the most. For him it was fun, without him realizing that it has a lot of benefits that's why we make sure that we find ways on how to incorporate more subjects to this activity to maximize its benefits.

Baking is one of the best ways to learn different skills and concepts across different subject areas. Concepts such as physical and chemical changes in matter, mixtures and solutions, and energy in Science; fractions, measurement, mathematical operations, and time in Mathematics; sight reading, reading comprehension, spelling, grammar, and communication in Reading and Language; "cleaning as you go (CLAYGO)", following instructions, sharing of food, appreciation of blessings, and the joy of learning and working in Values Education; and of course, the proper way of baking in Home Economics are few of the many things that Bunso may learn from baking.

Solving Puzzles from Small Parts to Whole

We are a family who practices minimalism and frugality. Our children imbibe these ways of living. They have this habit of not wanting more toys or things but when they do, we are so proud to say that they make the right choices. Less toys, less clutter. Most of the toys that are found here are toy cars, Gundam kits, Lego, Megabloks, and wooden educational puzzles. Most of them were given as gifts by our friends and family because they knew that our kids were fond of tinkering toys.

Speaking of puzzles, Bunso has this habit of solving puzzles by putting the small pieces together and then putting those built little pieces together to build the whole. What we like about Bunso is that he is very patient in tinkering his puzzles and never gets frustrated when he does not solve them immediately. All he does is to start building them over again until he is able to solve them. If we need more patience in dealing with Bunso, he is also the one teaching us to be more patient.

Playing Online Educational Games

The pandemic has brought many challenges to everyone in our family. We have realized that home-based online learning (HBOL) has many perks and difficulties. For starters, it is hard to separate work-related tasks to household chores. We do not employ any house helper. All household chores are assigned to a specific member of the family. Serious concerns arise when online classes have started since all of us have online school tasks and work-related activities. We observed that Bunso was fond of puzzle activities and we also noticed that his capacity to remember sequences was quite good and we also noted that there was an increase in his comprehension and analytical skills and speed after we decided to allow him to install puzzle applications. Some of the apps that he played which looked simple but require tremendous memorization of sequence were *Dancing Line* (he played almost all the versions found in Google Play store), *Monument Valley*, *Flow*, *Bridges*, *Dots, Escape Game*, *Move the Block*, jigsaw puzzles, driving simulations, and racing games. It may look like we were only allowing him to play to give us some breathing space. To be honest at one point we wanted to use those online games for that purpose but when we noticed that there were visible benefits to him, we decided to integrate the games into the tasks and skills that were required for his homeschooling activities. For example, there were lessons that required him to arrange events in sequence. Sometimes the sequence of events required a series of steps for it to be accomplished. We tried asking him to do the *Flow* game first before we started the lesson. Afterwards we used it as a springboard for the written activity. For the most part, we utilized Bunso's fascination with the internet in most of his lessons. Economically, we had less waste since instead of printing lots of worksheets or activity sheets for the diagnostic and formative assessments for his subjects, he would do it online while we supervised his schooling.

While it is true that online games gave Bunso very visible improvements, we also noticed that there were subtle changes in his behavior. Like at times he exhibits impatience when he is performing a task. His therapist told us that children who share the same condition as Bunso has a very high tendency to be addicted to online games since it greatly stimulates their mind. We also came across such pronouncements from our readings of research articles and some books. Due to this, we created a structure or a schedule of his gaming and internet surfing time. Since it involved him, we allowed him to plan with us his schedule. Then we made sure that we set alarms for each activity so that he might be reminded of his task. As you probably read in the past chapters of this book, conditioning took time and consistent repetition. However, we noticed that unlike when he was younger, the time for him to adapt to the schedule lessened through time. When we tried to determine the cause of such change, we realized that our practice of talking to him in the evening before bedtime wherein we would discuss our expectations and his schedule for the following day might have contributed to such change. Like before we would go out or proceed with an activity that might disrupt his schedule, conditioning him worked really well for us.

Integrated Approach in Teaching Subjects (massage included)

Conventional teaching instructions did not suit Bunso since his focus was highly dependent on sensorial inputs. Lecture type instruction would work at times but expecting him to stay put for more than an hour was highly unlikely. For a time, chaos reigned during lesson time. There were numerous occasions when most of us in the household became frustrated due to the stress brought about by Bunso's tantrums that mixed with the rising voices of the one teaching and the members of the household who were either complaining or were trying to control the situation. We were frustrated and tired until we came across an internet article about "*sensory integration*" wherein most of the inputs perceived by the senses could become a precursor for an intended course of action or reaction. To be honest, we literally experimented on Bunso. We tested which type of stimulation might allow him to focus or calm down. After many heartaches, tantrums, meltdowns, and small triumphs, we were able to determine that he would calm down whenever we would give him a hard massage. Furthermore, we also noticed that he would become more receptive when we would use manipulatives in his lessons. Added to this, he would respond more to auditory input than visual instructions. Although as time went on, his visual skills also developed. What was very observable to Bunso was his very sharp memory. We theorized that his ability to remember things probably was due to his *echolalia*, which is one of the characteristics of children with autism, and *palilalia* a condition wherein a person involuntarily repeats words, phrases, and sentences. We observed that he would literally repeat the entire lesson, story, and instruction of the things that we taught him.

With all our observations on Bunso's sensory issues and his manner of learning things, we used all his strong points whenever we would plan the execution of his lessons. One of the key points in all the strategies that we designed back then was the importance of giving him a body massage early in the morning. Upon waking up we would spend 10 to 20 minutes in cuddling him. As we cuddle him in bed and as we talk to him while giving him the massage, we would set the expectations for the day for all the activities that he would be doing. We would also discuss the schedule and the probable changes (This is very important because it allows us to change or insert other activities that might be important on the spur of the moment.). Most of his performance tasks, projects, and even assessments were designed to fulfill his sensorial needs. Tactile activities such as cutting, tracing, listening to a story, painting, counting using sticks, marbles, stones, Lego pieces, and even chocolate chips were used. Lessons were all integrated.

Example, when we taught him chemical and physical change, physical and chemical reaction, proper food handling and storage, importance of soap and hand washing, being thankful for the food that we eat, maximizing the use of resources, use of measuring tools, fractions, and phases of matter, we used baking. Every time we would bake his preferred cookies, chocolate cake, and cheese cupcakes we would talk about the lessons.

In teaching Bunso, we have to constantly think out of the box. Despite our limitations, we always find ways to search, device, and try new ways to conquer obstacles. Failure is never an option.

Use of Tactile Activities

We do not know when Bunso shall overcome the challenges of his condition. What we do now is what we believe can determine his future. All the activities that we give him is always anchored on research, articles, and books pertaining to ASD. This makes us confident that as his parents, teachers, and primary caregivers, we give what is best for him in our own simple but meaningful way.

We do our best to expose Bunso to different life adventures, it may be outside or in the comfort of our small home. We encourage him to do what he loves and discover the beauty of every endeavor even if he does not like some of them. We always tell him in the simplest way that in life, there are things that he does not like to do but he has to do them because they are necessary. We give him tasks to teach him the value of being responsible. We do not spoon feed him. We expose him to the outside world by teaching him how to commute and become street smart. We let him see that the world he lives in is not just about what is beautiful and comfortable but of course, there are harsh realities that he needs to see in order for him to value what he has and to find ways on how to live responsibly not just for his own sake but to coexist with others harmoniously as well. It is challenging to do at this point but we know that it is doable. We are looking forward to the day when he lives independently,

As parents, we value virtues and relationships more than material things. We prioritize practicing being good citizens more than being vain and focused on titles. We want people to treat us for who we are and not for what we have and this is what we always remind Kuya and Bunso to be.

When the pandemic ends, we will go back to exploring the different parts of our community, maybe the entire Philippines, and perhaps some parts world. Exposure to people and their backgrounds are two of the best ways to learn. Learning or discovering new things and different cultures beyond the eyes can see matters to us and we want to pass it to our kids. For me, learning to be appreciative of a person's background and culture as well as being empathic in his condition are the things that truly matter.

"Train up a child in the way he should go; even when he is old, he will not depart from it."

Proverbs 22:6

Chapter 5: Vigilance
by Papa Hector

"Consistency, belief, and constant vigilance to engage may have made a difference."

- Hector Martin Valdez

When Bunso was diagnosed with autism, we agreed in the family that we would do the same things that a normal family should do even with his condition. The way we approached things like discipline, nutrition, routines, and family traditions were patterned after our own family set-up. The usual things like going to church every Sunday, doing family bonding together, eating out once in a while, and other stuff were some of the things that we did. We thought Bunso would probably mature and learn to cope if we would expose him to our ways. Well, what we realized years later that living with autism might entail creating a unique family atmosphere and mindset to attain a certain degree of "normalcy" in the family. Attaining this would need constant and consistent "vigilance". We would usually remind each other jokingly that we were similar to a light sensor or a security system that could detect any anomaly in our surroundings.

Bunso's Occupational Therapist (OT) has always emphasized to us that children with autism for some reason have the tendency to exhibit different fixations and behavior based on a particular or prevalent experience that they are presently having. Two years after Bunso's diagnosis, we noticed his rigidity in following his preferred routines. A slight deviation from his routine back then could lead him to be agitated which at times would culminate into a tantrum or a total meltdown. His meltdowns, tantrums, repetitive actions, and fixations at times were always triggered by sensory stimuli. Like for instance, he would kiss each family member goodbye not just when we would go out of the house but also when we would go to the bathroom, to the pantry, and even the laundry area. It was very sweet but at times it became tiring due to the repetitive action. The most amusing part of it was when we were in need to go to the washroom to relieve ourselves. Even if we sneaked out, he would know and he would knock at the door and he would not stop until he was able to kiss us. Such fixation was triggered by a habit of kissing him before we go to work. He thought that every time we go out of the bedroom, that we should kiss him. He also had this fixation and routine on were to sit during meals, what utensils must be used on a particular dish, there was also the fixation of always checking on our "pantry" every time he would pass by the area. Then there was the turning on and off of light switches.

Vigilance does not apply to Bunso only. It also applies to us. Since Bunso is hypersensitive to sounds (Auditory Perception Disorder), we have developed the habit of toning down our voices during our conversations. Laughing out loud is not allowed as much as possible. Would you believe that the volume of our television is so low that we have given up on watching English movies and instead switched to Kdrama since we don't need to listen to the conversations because it comes with a subtitle? In fact, there was one time when some of our friends were watching a drama that we already watched at home, we were surprised to know that the soundtrack of the movie was actually good and that the music that was being played in our workplace was its soundtrack. We have learned to adjust and adapt immediately with Bunso's present fixations. We have noticed that by doing it, we can help Bunso adjust. We have also observed that he became more receptive to us.

Children with autism have a very low sense of danger. Due to this, we decided to be very attentive to his needs. There was a time when Bunso was very curious about "electric sockets". His curiosity was triggered when he saw us plugging some appliances. For the rest of us in the house, plugging an appliance was a common thing. Kuya, since he was six years older than Bunso, was already independent enough to perform most of the tasks at home on his own. Bunso, being very fond of his brother, saw his Kuya plug his tablet for charging. By the way, the tablet PC was the "in thing" during that time. Afterwards, Bunso started bugging us to "plug" and "unplug" the appliances around the house. We were mortified when he started doing it on his own even without our supervision. What made us worry so much was due to Bunso's disregard to his safety. For example, there was a time when we saw him plugging something while his hands were still wet. In fact, he was slightly electrocuted while doing it. During that time, our immediate reaction was to use his small mishap as a "teachable moment". We immediately gave reminders to him on the safety protocols to follow when he plugs and unplugs appliances. We also explained to him in a very calm and reassuring manner what caused the danger and how he could avoid it. We still remind him constantly of the safety procedures every time he does the act. Constant vigilance in ceasing many teachable moments is probably one of the key points in allowing us to reinforce Bunso's understanding of his surroundings.

    We have noticed that despite Bunso's condition, he is very receptive with his environment but his condition has prevented him to express in words his feelings and perception on the various events occurring around him. Furthermore, even the concept of pain is somewhat vague to Bunso. There was one time in 2019 that we saw him having difficulty walking on his way to the washroom to urinate. When we asked him why he was walking with a limp. He just looked at us and said "Kasi… I don't know." We asked him to sit on a stool and inspect his foot. We found out that one of his toes was infected. When the swollen toe was pressed, he said "It's ouch, Mama!" Only then did we realize that the concept of pain was vague to him. At that time, he was very verbal already so we thought that he might be able to pretty much describe what he felt. Due to that incident, we have become more observant on how Bunso would express what he feels. And true enough, we realized that many of the things that he experienced with his body were vague to him. We took the time to slowly explain the sensations or feelings that he experienced for a particular stimulus. For example, every time he ate, we would ask him to describe the taste. By the way since Bunso has difficulty creating coherent sentences, we always begin with a question, then followed by a "guide sentence or phrase then he fills in the rest, "Bunso, how does your food taste?" We always begin with his name to call his attention. Then it is followed by a leading sentence that goes like this, "My food is (descriptive word for the taste)." Then we repeat the process. Afterwards, we explain in very simple terms the reason why it is such or reinforce the learning by summarizing the things that he must remember. "Bunso, the cake is sweet because we added sugar to it. Remember sugar is sweet." This is usually punctuated by relating his new learning to his previous experiences by a synthesis question, "Bunso, can you give me things that you have eaten that is sweet?" From time to time during conversations, we recall events that happened in the past and we reinforce the learnings that he had in the past. Added to this, we see to it that we ask him to describe and relate to us his experiences. We always anchor it to what he is presently doing or an activity that he did the previous day. The technique on how we taught Bunso to reason out was shared to us by his Developmental Pediatrician. In one of our visits to her clinic, she told us that we could teach Bunso how to reason out by teaching him the reason why things happen. Since children with autism do mirroring and they also exhibit echolalia and palilalia, when we teach Bunso the reason why things happen, we also ask him to repeat or echo the reason to us.

Looking back, the habit of asking our words to be echoed to us has become so ingrained in our routine that we even exercise it when we teach our students and converse with our friends. Little by little as time went on, we are able to separate our habits between Bunso and our other roles. Up to now we still do it whenever we converse with Bunso. What we have realized is that Bunso has learned to reason out and it has come naturally. Right now, he still follows the format of presenting his reason out of habit. The habit of providing reason for things that he has observed and experienced has become a common form of expression. Many of our friends sometimes say that we are probably wrong to say that Bunso has autism. Many of them have told us that if our son has autism, how come he can reason out? It is something that is not usually observed in children with autism.

Our only dream back then when he was diagnosed was to have a meaningful conversation with him, to be able to hear him say words and repeat them, for him to tell us what he wants and be able to take care of himself. God gave us more than that. At the moment, Bunso is so "talkative" to a point where we can ask him to slow down sometimes. His reasoning is still not that perfect but as time goes on, his exposure to media, people, and his surroundings deepen. To our surprise, he has learned to be more observant and interactive with his surroundings which has enabled him to come up with his own conclusion. At one point, a friend of ours once asked us how we were able to do it. Our reply was "We were lucky to meet people who provided us with insights that changed our perspective. We changed our perspective, did our routines consistently, and continuously believe that Bunso can do it". Consistency, belief, and constant vigilance to engage with Bunso may have made a difference.

"Trust in the Lord with all your heart and lean not on your own understanding.

In all your ways submit to Him and He will make your paths straight."

Proverbs 3:5-6 NIV

Chapter 6: Resilience
by Papa Hector

"Resilience is very different than being numb. Resilience means you experience, you feel, you fail, you hurt. You fall. But, you keep going."

- Yasmin Mogahed

Living with autism has led us to see our lives in a different perspective. Most conventional beliefs anchored on the cultural standards in raising a child and maintaining a family may not apply to our set-up. Constructs such as love, understanding, and acceptance have more profound operational definition due to the experiences that we live by. Bunso's peculiarities brought about by him having Mild Autism with Attention Deficit Hyperactivity Disorder (ADHD), placed us in so many "awkward" situations. There was a time during one of our trips to the supermarket, he had a meltdown in the middle of the dispatching area. He was shouting at the top of his lungs while rolling on the floor. There was also an instance wherein while he was having a tantrum in the food court of a mall, an old lady approached and reprimanded us regarding our son's behavior. There was also the time when the security personnel of the mall asked us about our relationship with him. At that time, "mall abductions" was rampant. Furthermore, during kiddy parties, Bunso would stay outside of the venue. He would refuse to go inside and would just sit outside and afterwards he would tell us that he wanted to go home. When we dine in a restaurant, he would only order ice cream, spaghetti, and fries. The catch was that when he was done with his food, he would stand up from his chair and would immediately leave the restaurant. Whether we were done with our food or not was not important. He would just walk out.

Moreover, in the house, laughing and talking aloud is highly discouraged. The term "leisure walk" or "window shopping" does not exist in our vocabulary since all our "walks" always end up as "marathons". Kidding aside, when we reminisce those years when Bunso was still very sensitive to sensorial stimulation, we remember those moments when he was rolling on the floor while everyone in the vicinity were watching and those instances when we were approached by the supermarket security due to Bunso's howls and shouts. We always remember those times when we would agree to take a stroll at the mall to unwind and we end up very, very tired because we were running after Bunso.

Other than our struggles with Bunso's fixations and sensory problems, we also encountered ridicule from people in our community. There was a time when we received a summons from the security office of the place where we were living. Upon answering the summons, we were informed that a certain homeowner lodged a complaint that apparently Bunso allegedly threw a plastic bottle half filled with liquid to her husband from the window of our home. We were told that they were going to conduct an investigation regarding the complaint. We gave our consent to the investigation that they proposed. During the investigation, we were interviewed for our statement. After they were done with the investigation and learned of Bunso's condition, the security office told us that the allegation by the homeowner against our son was baseless. Afterwards, we sought an audience with the complainant in the presence of the security personnel. During our dialogue with the complainant, we asked her "What made her certain that it was Bunso who threw the bottle?" Her reply was "'Yong anak mo 'yon kasi may diprensya! (That was your son because he's crazy!)" At that time, it took us every ounce of patience and self-control not to berate the person. It was truly a very frustrating experience. Our frustration was borne from the discrimination that Bunso received and from the utter ignorance and lack of humanity of the complainant.

My father who is fondly called by Bunso as "Lolo Tatay" has always reminded us to be resilient. He has emphasized to us that rectifying the person or getting even with her is a total waste of time. We realized that getting even may sound good or would feel good but then it would never solve the problem. Due to this, we decided to be more receptive to Bunso's needs at the same time the members of our household became more vigilant in finding solutions to Bunso's fixations and other peculiarities. We came into a firm resolution that whatever problem we might encounter due to Bunso's peculiarities brought about by his condition, we would find a solution and that we would focus only on him and not mind how people around us think. Our resolution back then enabled us to be more proactive and accepting of our family's realities. Our resilience led to continuously rise-up to the challenge and in return made us better people. We could not change how people think but we definitely succeeded in changing our perspective to be more accepting and open minded.

Our personal and familial goals may have changed but it is also apparent that we can build other dreams and aspirations. Our success may not be up to the societal standards for success but it does not matter since we definitely are not on the same page. Our focus and gauge for success cannot be measured by monetary standards but rather it is anchored on the degree of our dedication, level of resilience, and unwavering faith in our beliefs and to the Creator. Solutions rather than problems, calculated action and not inaction, and embracing our fears and uncertainty for Bunso's future with his brother and accepting our responsibilities made us stand up and forge ahead without regrets.

"For I am the LORD your God who takes hold of your right hand and says to you, do not fear; I will help you."

Isaiah 41:13

Chapter 7: Gratitude
by Mama SJ

"A joyful life is not a floodlight of joy. A joyful life is made up of joyful moments gracefully strung together by trust, gratitude, inspiration, and faith."

- Brene Brown

Our family is not used to celebrating birthdays or special occasions by throwing huge parties. We are not comfortable having these maybe because Papa and I both belong to families that prefer intimate celebrations. During Bunso's fourth birthday, we prepared something simple that we thought would make him feel very special. We let Kuya plan the entire "surprise simple birthday party" not just because he insisted but we wanted him to use his creativity to show his little brother how he really cared.

On the day before the celebration, Kuya showed us the birthday card that he was making for Bunso. He was so excited to tell us that he started doing it during his free time in school and he would still do the finishing touches later. While he wasn't looking, I asked Papa, "Did you tell him to do that?" Then he said he didn't. I was so touched. How sweet of Kuya!

Kuya continued decorating the birthday card diligently. Right after finishing it, he handed it to us and said, "I know that Bunso doesn't know how to read yet. Will you keep this for me? When he knows how to read, can we show this to him?" I couldn't help myself but cry while reading Kuya's message and laughed out loud thereafter. I hugged him and said, "Thank you, Kuya! You're such a sweet brother. Bunso will surely love and appreciate this. When the time comes that he knows how to read and understands what you mean, we will be showing this to him definitely."

The following day, we mentioned to Bunso upon waking up that it was his birthday (at this point, he wasn't scared yet when he would hear the words "Happy Birthday") and Papa and Kuya would have a surprise upon arrival in the afternoon. He patiently waited and he was very sad because the boys went home late. His sadness faded away and he jumped with joy when he saw the small chocolate cake and Pancit Bilao that they were carrying. We set up our dining table, prepared the food, and sang the Birthday Song, and ate together as a family. While doing so, we could see in Bunso's eyes how happy he was! For a child who could barely talk and express his emotions, his smile said it all and it was indeed priceless!

After our simple feast, Kuya showed his first gift, a shape sorter, and Bunso opened the box quickly. He was so excited to play with it. When he felt bored, Kuya handed him his second gift, a ball. If Bunso was happy receiving his first gift, on this one he was more excited! He was not yet capable of expressing his gratitude and longing towards his brother and I was glad that Kuya didn't wait anymore for his little brother to say, "Thank you" and initiated to play with him immediately without being told to do so.

I watched blissfully as my two boys played together with their Papa. I felt so proud of Kuya for doing the best of his ability to plan Bunso's birthday party and for making him happy despite not being sure how his brother would reciprocate the time and effort that he exerted in that thoughtfulness of his.

This happened seven years ago. Kuya was nine that time. As days, months, and years passed, I realized that Kuya was digesting most if not all, the advice that Papa and I were giving him--- to make other people happy and to become good, generous, understanding, and caring to others especially to his little brother. We saw a lot of improvements with Bunso in terms of his behavior and Kuya was the big factor in those milestones. For that, we are truly grateful.

From that day on, living with a family member with autism becomes very challenging everyday but we learn how to celebrate life not just during special occasions but anytime, everywhere daily. We appreciate simple things, joys, triumphs, milestones, blessings, and even trials that come our way. We believe that there is always beauty in everyday no matter how bad the situation it seems. We learn to be more patient, forgiving, understanding, trustful, and loving. We become more generous of our time with one another especially with Bunso who needs it the most.

We extend our efforts in all aspects. We do our best to become the best version of ourselves. We are contented with what we have but never contented with who we are. Our family life is not perfect but we always see beauty in that imperfection. Oprah Winfrey once said, "The more you praise and celebrate your life, the more there is in life to celebrate." It's happening. It's so true. There is always a reason to be grateful and happy.

Before Bunso was born, it was easier for us to make decisions because Kuya grew up independent and free-willed. Papa and I were focused on planning for our family's future to give ourselves the life that we deserve. We would always work on our long-term goals, do hustling, and perhaps missed so many moments that we thought insignificant at the moment. Then Bunso came when Kuya was six years old. It was a 360 degree turn and there was a sudden change in our plan of levelling up our career path and putting it aside instead. We learned how to live slowly and intentionally. We realized that life was just fleeting and we should never exchange wonderful memories with things that fade away. We literally started over again because for the longest time, Kuya was our only child. The adjustment period was quite challenging and most of all, our finances became unstable due to Bunso's basic and special needs. It was never easy raising two kids in this generation but as days passed by, the happiness that Bunso brought to our family could never be equated with money. It was the same feeling that we had when Kuya came into our lives. What made it different was there were two kids who were giving us so much happiness and purpose.

Bunso was such a blessing to our family, our second bundle of joy, our source of strength and grit. He gave us a different perspective on things and made us better parents and individuals. Some might say that his condition was giving us pressing moments but on the contrary, by just a mere presence of him, all the hardships would fade away.

Bunso is the one who has taught us the habit of gratitude, to be thankful for all the blessings right in front of us and those that are soon to come. We have learned to appreciate little things more and become aware of what truly matters. We have learned how to value every milestone even though how simple they may be. Counting our blessings and being thankful always keep us see the goodness behind

Bunso's condition. We are so blessed that we are surrounded with good people who are there to support us. There are also strangers who come our way on the right place at the right time to lighten our load. They keep us motivated to move forward because they have made us see that there is hope, that Bunso may change and improve little by little in God's time. There was a person who led us to a special school and occupational therapy center right after Bunso's diagnosis and there we found the best professionals who could help us. When we admitted that Bunso was diagnosed with Autism Spectrum Disorder (ASD), we were able to meet individuals who had the same situation as ours and they became our source of support. We also met experts who could teach us to become equipped in parenting Bunso. Due to his needs, we became innovative and resourceful and we were so blessed that a wide array of resources was readily available on the internet. The ways and means to guide us as autism parents were countless.

Practicing the habit of gratitude opens for more blessings to come in our family. In our own simple way, we may have the chance to give inspiration to other autism parents out there that it is not always a hindrance or a liability to have a child with ASD.

"Rejoice always, pray continually, give thanks in all circumstances, for this is God's will for you in Christ Jesus."

Thessalonians 5:16-18

Chapter 8: Where Are We Now?

Being Equipped Matters
by Mama SJ

"Every time I thought I was being rejected from something good, I was actually being re-directed to something better."

- Steve Maraboli

My Road to Professional Upgrading for Bunso

In October 2018, I decided to fulfill my dream of becoming a Special Education Teacher. My purpose was for self-fulfillment, to become a credible special education teacher and autism advocate, and most of all to become the best teacher for Bunso. I felt inadequate as an autism mom for five years and I wanted to learn more. I listed down the schools where my son's former teachers graduated because they exuded excellence. My inspiration was to have the same competencies. Then I met an illustrious teacher, the graduate school dean of the school where I first inquired. When she saw my last school attended where I took my Bachelor of Science in Nursing as a third course and my current situation as a stay-at-home-mom, she told me to stop filling-in the application form and said…

"Tatapatin kita (Frankly speaking), I can't accept you because I don't want our school to be tainted with a school with bad reputation."

"Bakit doon ka pumasok kasi madalian lahat? (Did you study there to make it easier on your part?)"

"Hindi mo kakayanin dito. (You cannot make it here.)"

She didn't even bother to take a look on my transcript of records. I explained to her the stories behind every course that I took, that I loved learning, and I wasn't a mediocre student but she wasn't interested at all. I felt discriminated but that rejection led me to call the next school on my list. I was able to talk to a nice lady, Ma'am Christine Santos of Arellano University Graduate School of Education, the following day. I cried when she answered *"Oo naman, bakit naman hindi? (Yes, of course. Why not?)"* in my question, *"Do you accept students who graduated from PCHS?"* Afterwards, I met her and an equally nice and inspiring teacher, the late Dr. Federico Castillo, who interviewed me. As expected, I cried again during the interview.

I have learned that "Arellano University welcomes all students interested in the pursuit of scholarly learning, regardless of race, creed, religion, and personal circumstances." Isn't it amazing? The road to my success there might be challenging but the community has embraced and supported me with open arms that make my stay worthwhile.

I am thankful that I was accepted as a student there. It is a blessing to hone my skills and acquire new knowledge in an institution who treats my family as part of its community. If not for Arellano University and my professors, I may not have the guts to have my journal entries about my "autism mom journey" to be written in a book.

Our Decision to Pull Out Bunso from School and Homeschool Him Instead

As teachers, Papa and I always believe in the passion of each one. Sadly, we have observed that what our government's system lacks right now is the capacity to appreciate and empower the skills and talents of the ones teaching and learning in the classroom which has led to our family's decision to homeschool Bunso while feeling that I was ready to take over as his teacher. We realized that the design of the curriculum apparently was not designed for kids with special needs. The program was more focused on academic skills rather than life skills despite following an Individualized Education Plan (IEP).

Although the teachers and therapists were good, we saw "learning gaps" that needed to be addressed. The reason why we decided to homeschool Bunso was not about the teachers and therapists. They were family. They were good, passionate, and compassionate. They contributed positively for who Bunso is right now. It was the nationwide education system that made us decide to take over our son's mode of learning.

Added to this, we think the problem with the present school curriculum are: a) There is so much bureaucracy; b) It may be inferred through observation that the curriculum design is not developmentally-appropriate; c) There is so much stuff to teach yet so little time for skills mastery; and d) We are technically educating students who don't even know what and how they study and why they are studying such concepts. Come to think of it, if the curriculum and schools are functioning properly for every child and if the energy of teachers are focused on teaching what is necessary, we think that we don't need to homeschool Bunso anymore. Putting our reflection in two statements, we would say that…

"If you are willing to learn, a concerned teacher can help you. If you are determined to learn, a compassionate teacher can guide you."

"A teacher rooted in his purpose will never discriminate but rather, seek for that teachable moment."

As teachers and educators, we believe that we must never forget that learning is rooted on the basics and foundations of our students anchored on a strong sense of morality. Students' holistic success is determined by not how many lessons they have been taught but rather by how they use them to improve themselves more and be progressive and conscientious learners.

"A teacher teaches a student the things to do and remember while an educator teaches a student how to learn and why he is learning."

As teachers and educators, Papa and I commit to seek teachable moments in a learner and always remember our role as teachers by knowing our learners because a teacher or an educator should be the number one learner. This is also our first step in parenting our children especially Bunso who has ASD. We always make sure to inject teachable moments in every conversation we make with our children and every person that we meet. We teach and lead by example so that our children and the people that we meet will realize their purpose anchored on humility, integrity, loyalty, love, and unquenchable thirst for knowledge, growth, and collaboration. We only live once and it is nice to leave a legacy focused on touching lives and empowering our children and other learners to be the best version of themselves.

My Musings as a Teacher and Autism Mom

As part of my pursuit in equipping myself to become a credible autism advocate and teacher to Bunso, reading published works like journals, research, and textbooks about special education and philosophy of education and reflecting on them are among the various tasks that my professors in the graduate school require us to do every semester. These endeavors are tasking but they help me become a better teacher.

Reflection on "My Pedagogical Creed by John Dewey"

John Dewey's declaration on education stressed five points: 1) True education may come from social situations revolving around societal norms that may be acquired from continuous interaction with the environment; 2) School is a social institution that reflects society and creates continuity of experience that may lead to gradual growth from home life to a deeper understanding of the rudiments of social interactions, facilitated and evaluated, not taught by the teacher; 3) The subject matter of the school curriculum may be anchored to activities that direct social integration to create meaningful interactions where the learner develops new attitudes, interests, and experience by creating synergy across academic disciplines; 4) The teaching method may be enhanced by providing the necessary stimuli to enhance the learner's capacity to visualize and feel their learning goals by providing activities that are within the interests of the learner; and 5) The school must guide the learner to live the spirit and ideals of the institution through shared social consciousness.

My experiences in teaching Bunso who was diagnosed with *Mild Autism Spectrum Disorder* made him quite detached to his surroundings so my husband and I focused on entering his world then afterwards he became part of ours. Though in the beginning we were actually not sure if it was going to work, we noticed that through his exposure, he would continuously acquire just like everybody the norms within his environment and it allowed him to blend in. Then his former school was informed at the same time we involved ourselves in the development and implementation of his *Individualized Educational Plan (IEP)*. In doing so, we were able to create learning continuity that led us to homeschool him. We made sure that all concepts were incorporated to an actual activity. One example would be cooking which made use of Math, Science, History, and Art concepts. The integrated approach made him put together the related concepts into concrete understanding while we only facilitate the learning process.

As an educator and a parent, my passion in helping my son overcome his inadequacies compels me to continue innovating, find new solutions, utilize present strategies in creating unique approaches that will provide my son with the leverage to overcome his condition. Given this challenge, I have also committed to document and share our journey to many people via social media so that they may be inspired and informed or vice versa.

Reflection on "A Talk to Teachers by James Baldwin"

A Talk to Teachers by James Baldwin speaks about the following points: 1) The purpose of education is to motivate a person to examine his surroundings and enable himself to make willful decisions; 2) The primary aim of education is to capacitate the person to interact with the society as well as identifying his purpose in that place which in turn would empower him to live at peace with himself and find his own identity; and 3) Educational paradox is when a person begins to develop a conscience or independent thought when he can swiftly recognize the flaws of his society, change it for the better, and willingly fight for it no matter what the risk is.

When Bunso, who was diagnosed with *Autism Spectrum Disorder* attended formal schooling, my husband and I literally scoured for literature that might enable us to help him. After many considerations, we agreed back then that we would work towards making him able to make his own decisions and be self-reliant. We made sure that he would have a say on all our family activities. Now, he is able to create his own daily schedule, even at times when our own schedules are influenced by him. Our friends whenever they meet him cannot simply believe that he is highly sociable and is able to make his own decisions given his condition. Bunso has been labeled and judged at times due to his peculiar behavior and divergent perspective on things but he doesn't feel that he is different from the rest. He exudes confidence and lives happily no matter what society says or thinks about him because we treat him like a regular kid. His "core" is anchored in unconditional love, utmost acceptance, and learned virtues that's why he doesn't feel his inadequacies and he is ready to face society confidently despite its unfair judgment.

As an educator and mom, my eagerness to strengthen my child's self-reliance and self-directedness and to educate society regarding his condition has inspired me to pursue further studies in Special Education. This endeavor aside from learning from my journey as an "autism mom" gives me the credibility in educating people and spreading awareness about autism rooted on research and facts through meaningful conversions, both personally and online through sharing of articles, strategies, and success stories not just to impart pertinent information but to inspire teachers and parents of children with autism and other exceptionalities to show the world that children under our care are more than just their diagnosis.

Dreams Come True

In the book "The Secret by Rhonda Byrne", it is reiterated that "thoughts become things". What we desire: the things that we want to own, emotions that we want to feel, circumstances that we like to have, people that may help us to reach our goals every step of the way, are always drawn to us by God and the universe. Our utmost desire to share our autism journey not just to chronicle Bunso's milestones and our family's ups and downs along the process but to serve as lessons and inspiration is here. Papa and I pray that after reading this book, you may join us in advocating for people with ASD by simply being more understanding and open-minded when you meet a person or a family taking care of their loved one with ASD. If you are an autism parent like us, may the things that are working for us may also work for you and your child. God bless us all.

We are Spontaneous as Always
by Papa Hector

"Life is a series of natural and spontaneous changes. Don't resist them; that only creates sorrow. Let reality be reality. Let things flow naturally forward in whatever way they like."

- Lao Tzu

Six years flew by as if they were yesterday. You might be wondering "Where we able to conquer autism?" Our eternal answer to this question will always be "It is a work in progress." While it's true that autism does not have a cure "yet", our triumphs lie on the small steps that we have continuously taken together in making Bunso realize his potential while we also discover more of who we are as a person. My family and I may have experienced together bitter arguments, strenuous adjustments, broken dreams, simple joys, and triumphs, but at the end of the day we have learned more on the reasons why we love and forge our bonds together towards self-actualization. We have learned to grow together, push each other to be more proactive. "Tough love" probably may be an apt description to what we have. We learned to stand alone while relying on each other.

While writing this book, there were moments when we started asking ourselves "Can we really finish this book?" Do you know why? When we received the commission to write a book, problems and obstacles started popping up. My wife got sick the following day after we received the news. Then our landline and internet connection got disconnected one after the other. On top of that, school related matters made online classes very stressful since we had to rely on data connection for online classes for my sons, and for our respective work. But wait, there is more. Bunso who does online activities since he is homeschooled suddenly changed his routine. Before our connection was severed due to the line migration of the leading telephone company in the country, his online homeschooling lessons and activities pretty much occupied his entire mornings. Afternoons were allotted to online drills, and rest and recreation. Due to the internet dilemma, Bunso's routine got sidetracked, His response to the internet stimuli was to add more activities such more eating time (I think most of his time is spent on this.), more reading sessions as well as "cudle-cudle/tickle-tickle time". By the way, I forgot to mention that part of his sensory problem before was his inability to feel touch sensation. We were able to help him regain his sensations through body massage and would you believe "tickling". We also recently discovered that his "shouting or yelling" reaction whenever we accidentally raise the volume of our voices is his method of adapting to the stress brought about by his very sensitive sense of hearing. To be honest we were still wondering up until now how we were able to finish this project.

Anyway, as for our struggles with Bunso's condition we can say that right now we are thriving and still learning. Our simple wish of allowing us to hear him say some words and be able to look at us and recognize us as his parents have already been fulfilled. Every day is a gift. A present that was hard earned borne from the efforts and unselfish acts of so many people who are part of our journey. We continue to push each other to be better versions of ourselves every day. There is still uncertainty in the future, but we believe that the future is today. Our actions, decisions, and most of all conviction and faith to live each day without regrets may forge a future which may be better than what we have envisioned. This book is a simple record of our journey of discovery, struggles, and hard-earned triumphs to conquer an adversary that we cannot see but has a profound effect on the very foundation of our family. I always ask our Father Almighty that if it is possible that no family or child may experience the very difficult and uncertain journey that most family of children with special needs undergo.

"Perhaps this is the moment for which you have been created."

Esther 4:14

Appendix

References

Books

Baldwin, J. (2008). A Talk to Teachers. In Provenzo, E. F. Jr. (Ed.), *Foundations of Educational Thought* (Vol. 2, pp. 107-112). USA: SAGE Publications Ltd.

Dewey, J. (2008). My Pedagogical Creed. In Provenzo, E. F. Jr. (Ed.), *Foundations of Educational Thought* (Vol. 1, pp. 195-203). USA: SAGE Publications Ltd.

Websites

A-Z Quotes | Quotes for All Occasions. (2021). A-Z Quotes. https://www.azquotes.com/

BibleGateway.com: A searchable online Bible in over 150 versions and 50 languages. (2015). Biblegateway.com. https://www.biblegateway.com/

Cambridge Dictionary | English Dictionary, Translations & Thesaurus. (2021, February 17). @CambridgeWords. https://dictionary.cambridge.org/

About the Authors

SHARON JOYCE S. VALDEZ also known as Mama SJ is a Licensed Professional Teacher; integrative learning, reading, and autism advocate; digital content creator; homeschooling mom; stay-at-home mom of two boys; and happy wife of an educator. She is frugal, practical, and minimalist. She believes that having a happy life does not need to be extravagant. She is into living intentionally and slowly, a mom who values the quality of life with her family more than anything else. What she writes about in her website and social media accounts speaks of her lifestyle and what she believes in which she wants to share with the world hoping that somehow people can learn something from.

She is currently a Master of Arts in Special Education candidate in Arellano University, Manila. She completed her B. S. Botany in University of Santo Tomas, Certificate in Teaching in Philippine Normal University, and B. S. Nursing in Philippine College of Health Sciences, Inc. She was a former grade school and early education teacher at Xavier School San Juan.

You may connect with her through her website and social media platforms.

Website: www.allaroundpinaymama.com
Facebook and Instagram: @allaroundpinaymama
Twitter: @multitasking_sj

Other book by Sharon Joyce Valdez:

Nanay, Nanay, Paano Maging Ina?
Natatanging Kwentong Mula sa Puso
(The Filipino Homemakers, 2019)

―――

HECTOR MARTIN I. VALDEZ also known as Paps or Papa Hector is a Licensed Professional Teacher and has been teaching in La Salle Green Hills Integrated School, Mandaluyong City (LSGHIS) for the past 20 years. He was a Science item-writing consultant at Center for Educational Measurement (CEM); module writer and achievement test writer for LSGHIS; guest lecturer at Shude School in Lian Jiang County, Fuzhou City, People's Republic of China; and Science textbook author for Salesiana Books by Don Bosco Press, Inc. He believes that all people have the capacity to excel in their own way and that learning is a lifelong journey of self-discovery and actualization. His most cherished dream and goal is to be an excellent father, husband, and son.

He is currently a Master of Arts in Educational Leadership and Management candidate at De La Salle University, Manila. He completed his B. S. Botany in University of Santo Tomas and Teacher's Certificate at De La Salle University, Manila.

You may connect with him at
hector.valdez@lsgh.edu.ph.

Other book by Hector Martin Valdez:
The Amazing World of Science Grade 5
(Salesiana Books by Don Bosco Press, Inc, 2011)

Made in the USA
Monee, IL
11 July 2021